CONTENTS

W9-CHP-539

HOW TO USE THIS BOOK
The Chord Diagram

The chords are displayed as diagrams that represent the fingerboard of the guitar. There are six vertical lines representing the six strings of the guitar. Horizontal lines represent the frets. The strings are arranged with the high E (first, or thinnest) string to the right, and the low E (sixth, or thickest) to the left. The black circles indicate at which fret the finger is to be placed and the number tells you which finger to use. At the top of the diagram there is a thick black line indicating the nut of the guitar. Above the chord diagram you will occasionally see X's and O's. An X indicates that the string below it is either not played or damped, an O simply means the string is played as an open string. A curved line tells you to bar the strings with the finger shown; that is, lay your finger flat across the indicated strings.

The fingerings in this book might be different from fingerings you have encountered in other chord books. They were chosen for their overall practicality in the majority of situations.

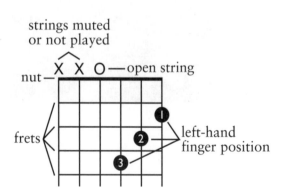

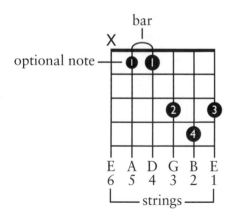

The Photo

The photo to left of each chord diagram shows you what your hand should look like on the guitar fingerboard.

Although the photos are a visual reference, all of the fingers in a given shot may not be in a proper playing position. We have sometimes moved unused fingers *out of the way,* to give you a better look at where the fretting fingers are placed. For instance, when playing the G♯m shown in the photograph below, the third finger should not be tucked under the neck, it would normally be relaxed and extended upward over the fingerboard. Make sure your fingers are comfortable and that you are capable of moving them easily from one chord position to another.

G♯m

TUNING THE GUITAR

The guitar can be tuned with the aid of pitch pipes or an electronic guitar tuner, which are available through your local music dealer.

If you do not have a tuning device you can use the relative tuning method.

Relative Tuning

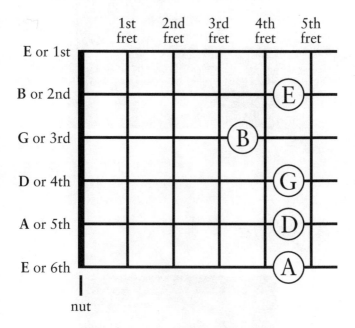

Press down where indicated, one at a time, following the instructions below.

Estimate the pitch of the 6th string as near as possible to E or at least a comfortable pitch (not too high, as you might break other strings in tuning up).

Then, while checking the various positions on the above diagram, place a finger from your left hand on: the 5th fret of the E or 6th string and **tune the open A** (or 5th string) to the note (A)

the 5th fret of the A or 5th string and **tune the open D** (or 4th string) to the note (D)

the 5th fret of the D or 4th string and **tune the open G** (or 3rd string) to the note (G)

the 4th fret of the G or 3rd string and **tune the open B** (or 2nd string) to the note (B)

the 5th fret of the B or 2nd string and **tune the open E** (or 1st string) to the note (E)

KEY OF C

C

C6

Cmaj7

C

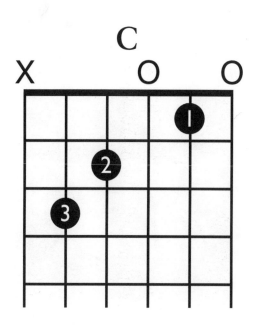

C6

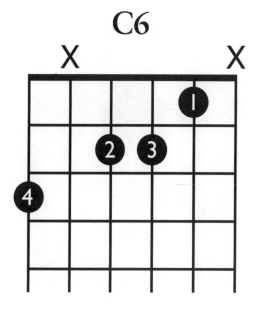

Cmaj7

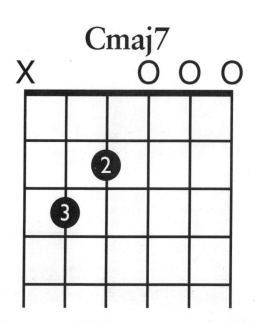

KEY OF C

Csus4

Dm

Em7

Csus4

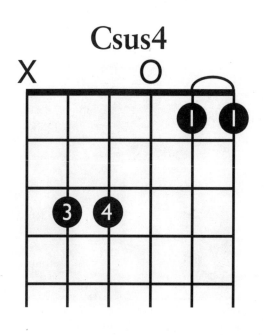

Dm

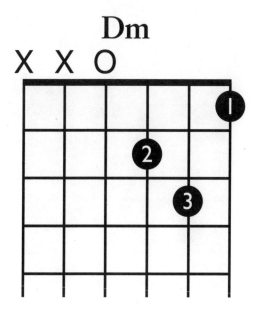

Em7

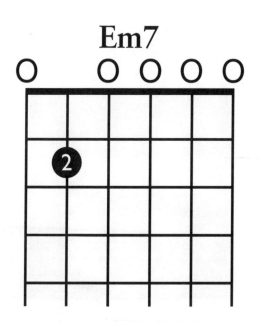

KEY OF C

F

G7

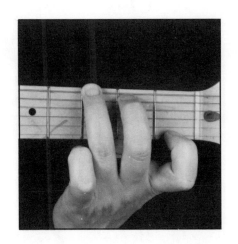

Am

F

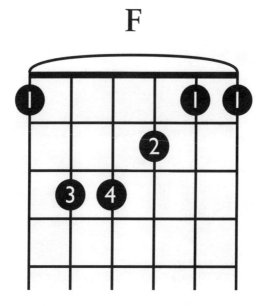

G7

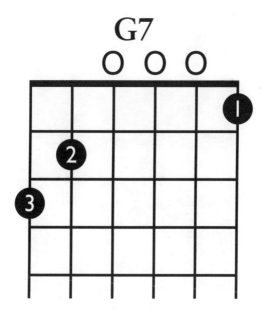

Am

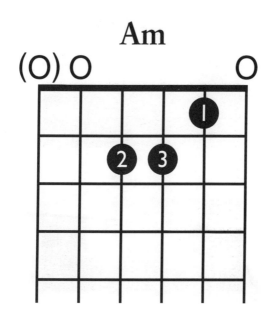

KEY OF D

D

D6

Dmaj7

D

X (O) O

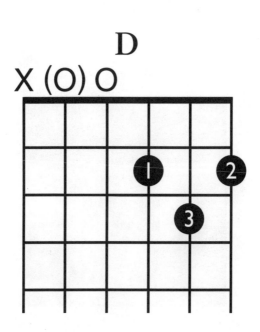

D6

X (O) O   O

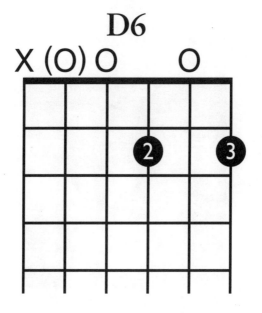

Dmaj7

X (O) O

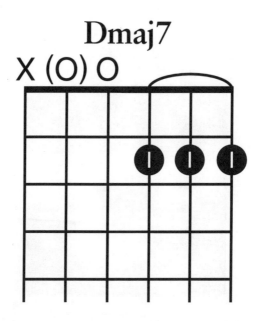

KEY OF D

Dsus4

Em

F#m

Dsus4

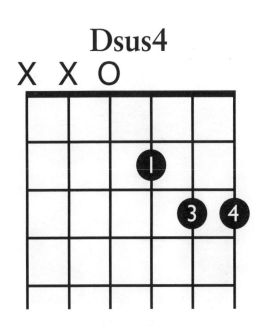

Em

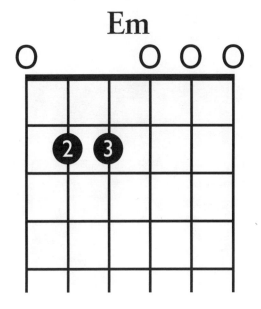

F#m

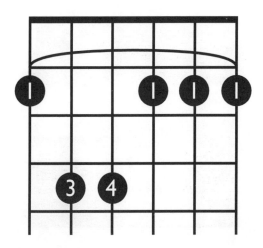

KEY OF D

G

A7

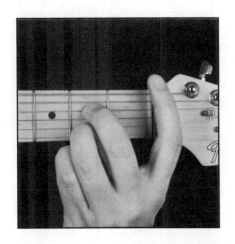

Bm

G

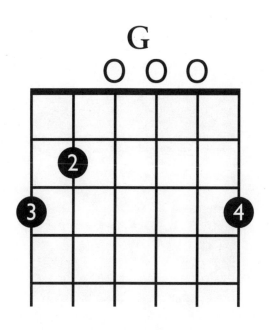

A7

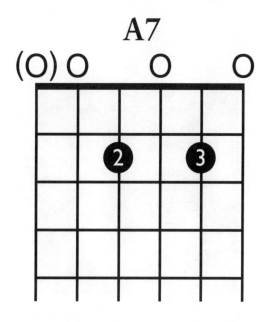

Bm

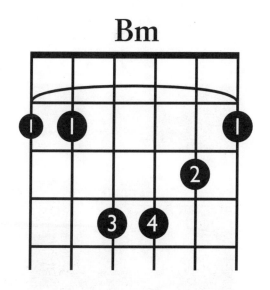

KEY OF E♭

E♭

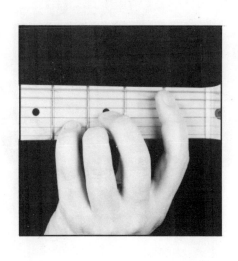

E♭6

E♭maj7

$E\flat$

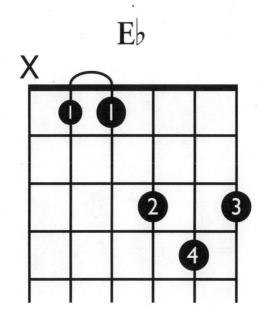

$E\flat 6$

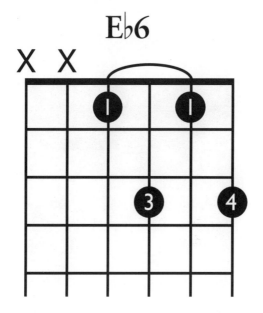

$E\flat maj7$

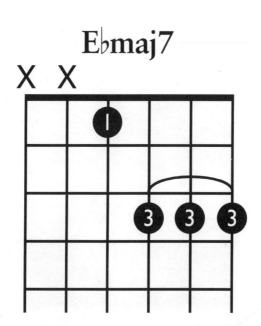

KEY OF E♭

E♭sus4

Fm

Gm

E♭sus4

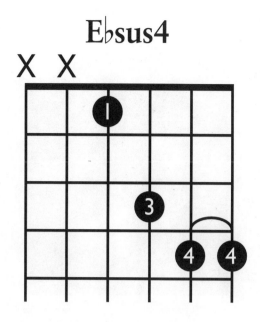

Fm

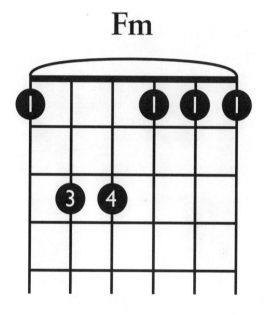

Gm

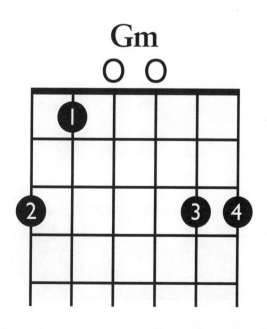

Key of E♭

A♭

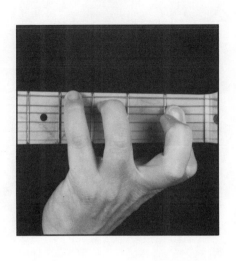

B♭7

Cm

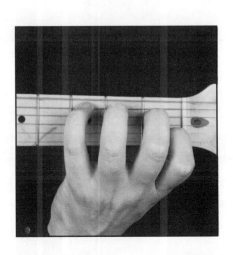

$A\flat$

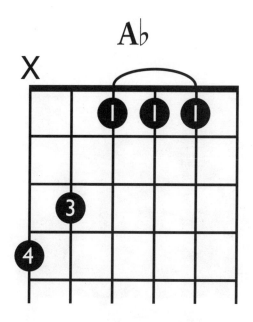

$B\flat7$

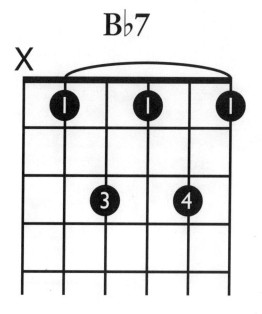

Cm

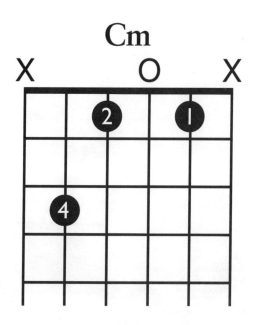

KEY OF E

E

E6

Emaj7

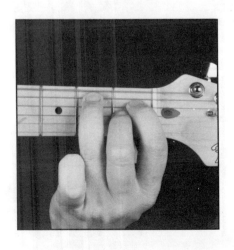

E

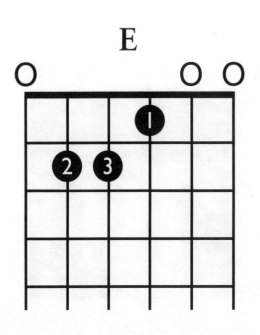

E6

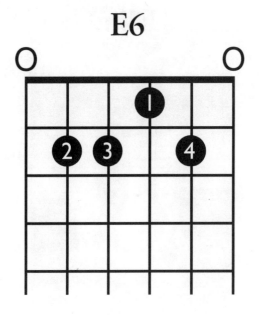

Emaj7

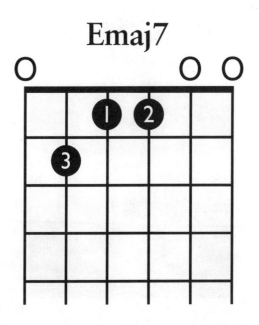

27

KEY OF E

Esus4

F#m

G#m

Esus4

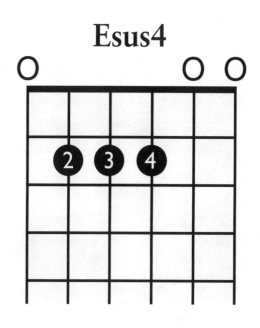

F#m

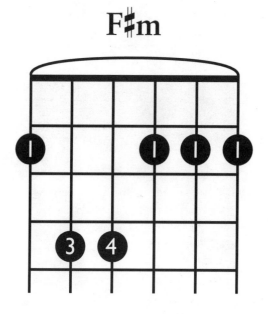

G#m

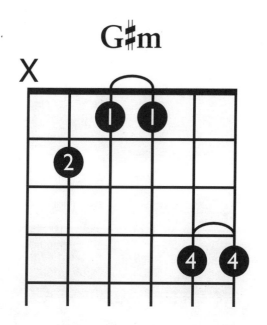

KEY OF E

A

B7

C#m

A

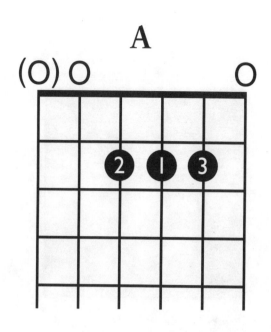

B7

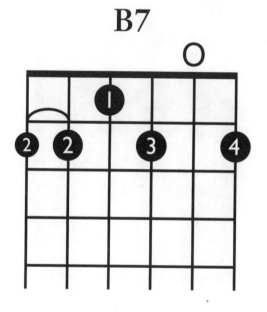

C#m

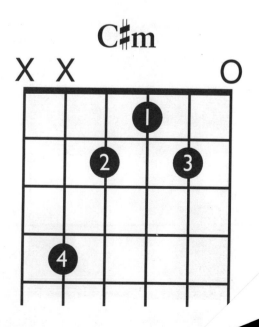

KEY OF F

F

F6

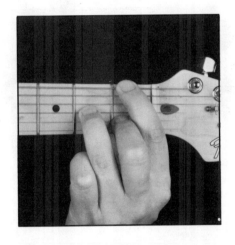

Fmaj7

A

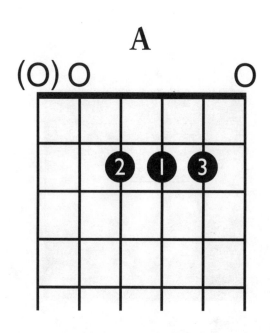

B7

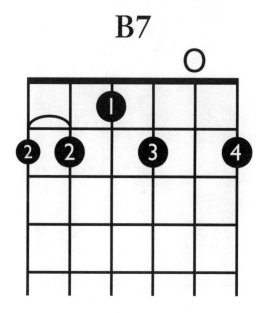

C#m

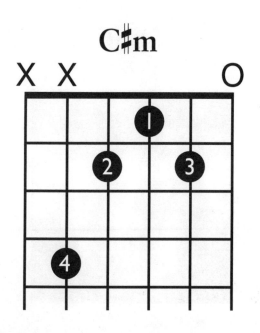

KEY OF F

F

F6

Fmaj7

F

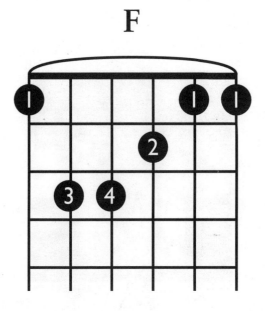

F6

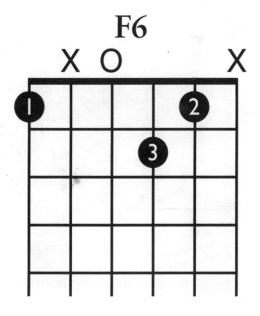

Fmaj7

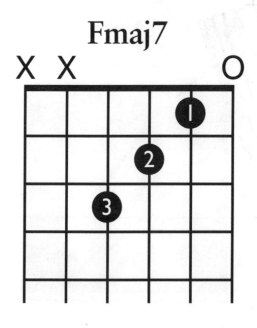

KEY OF F

Fsus4

Gm

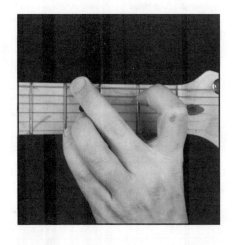

Am

Fsus4

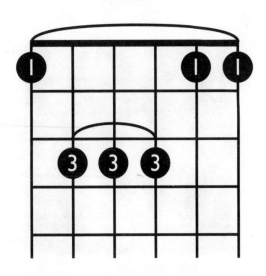

Gm

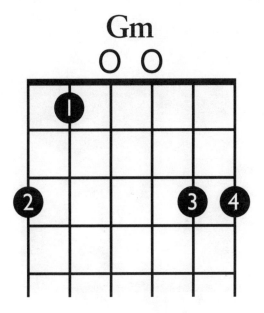

Am

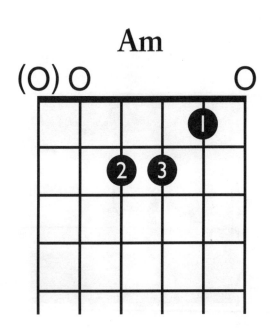

KEY OF F

B♭

C7

Dm

B♭

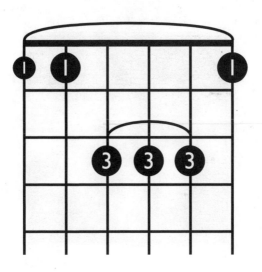

C7

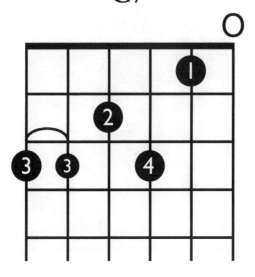

Dm

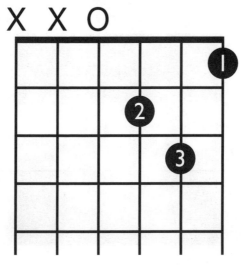

KEY OF G

G

G6

Gmaj7

G

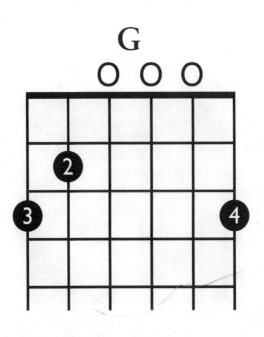

G6

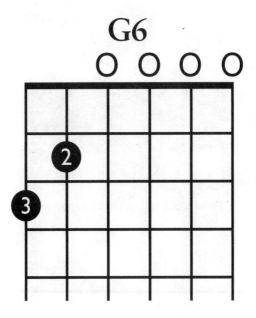

Gmaj7

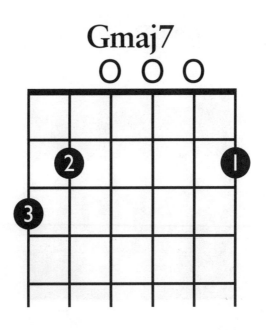

KEY OF G

Gsus4

Am

Bm

Gsus4

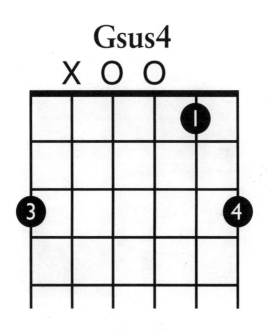

Am

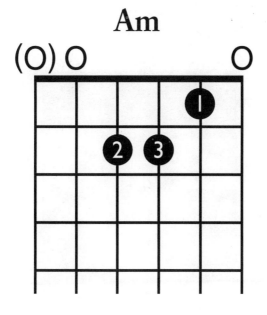

Bm

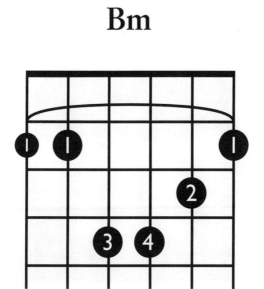

KEY OF G

C

D7

Em

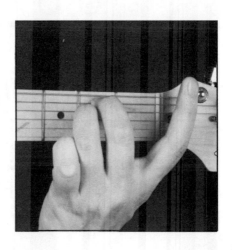

C

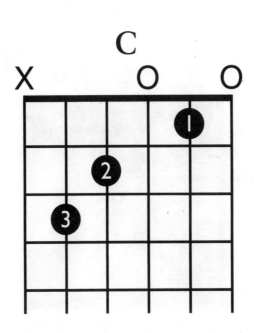

D7

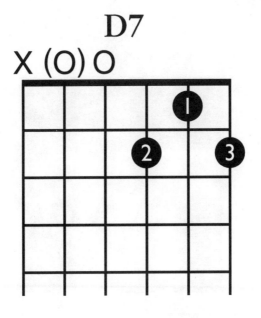

Em

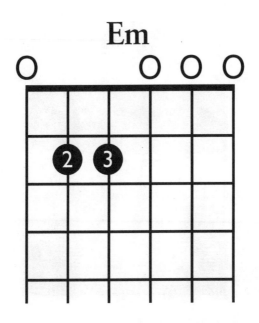

KEY OF A

A

A6

Amaj7

A

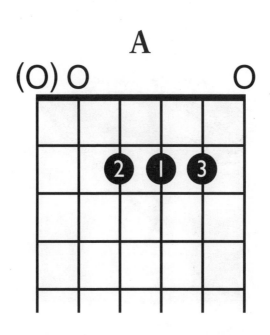

A6

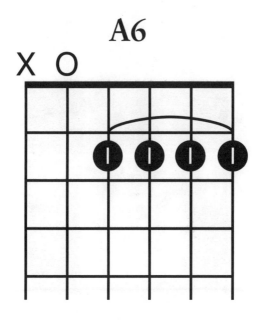

Amaj7

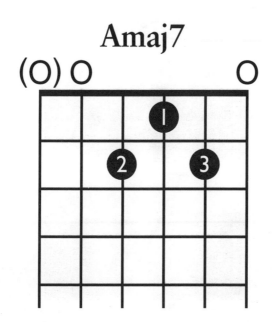

KEY OF A

Asus4

Bm

C#m

D

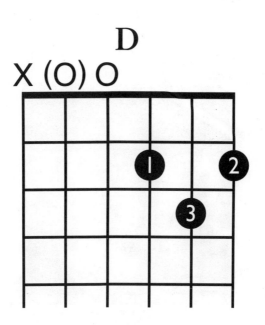

E7

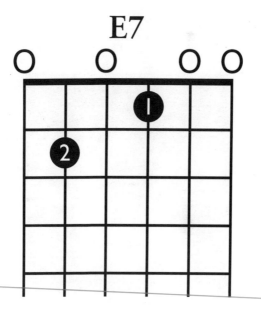

F#m7

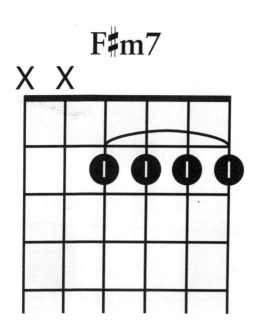

KEY OF B♭

B♭

B♭6

B♭maj7

B♭

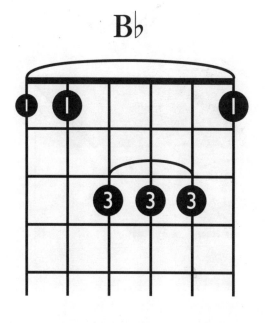

B♭6

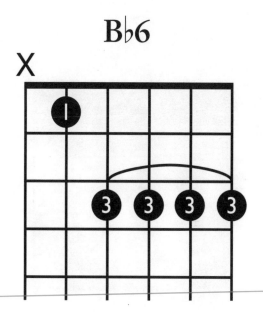

B♭maj7

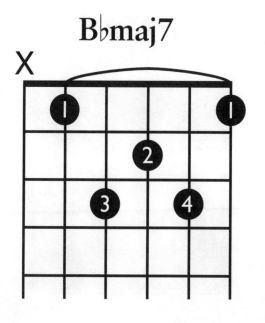

KEY OF B♭

B♭sus4

Cm

Dm

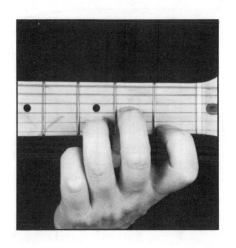

B♭sus4

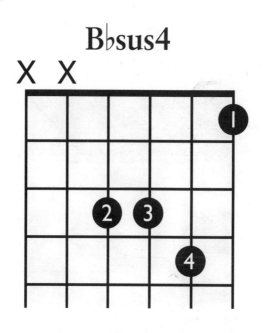

Cm

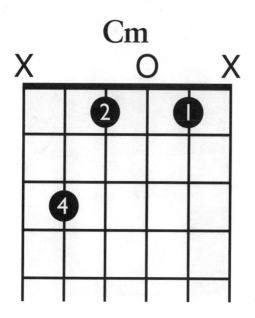

Dm

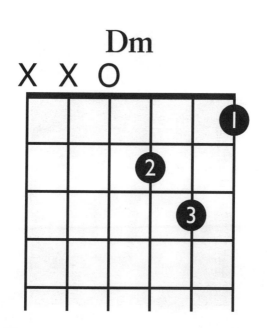

KEY OF B♭

E♭

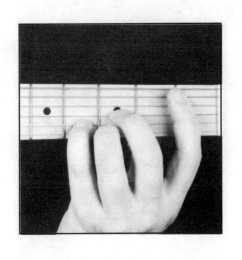

F7

Gm

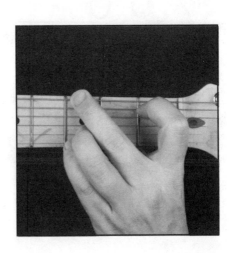

E♭

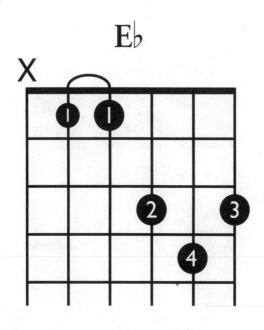

F7

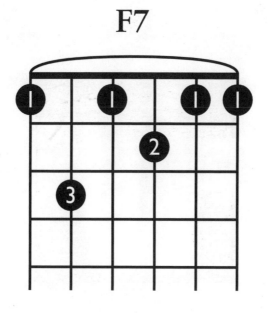

Gm

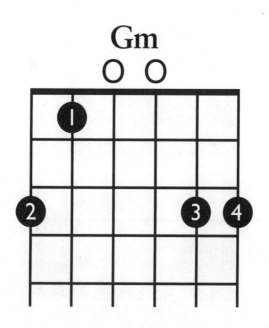